Retirement Devotional
By Robert Laura

D1496095

Dedication

This book would not be possible without the love
and support of my best friend and amazing wife
Amie, and our wonderful children. I love you Amie,
Connor, Ava, Lucas, and Drake. Words cannot
express what you mean to me and how blessed I
feel to have you in my life.

Table Of Contents

Introduction

Over the last 10 years, I have taken a very different retirement planning journey than most financial professionals because I felt called to apply a biblical lens to the world of retirement.

Now retirement is a popular and well-known topic that enters into a person's life when they start working and of course as the years go on, the topic becomes more and more important...and for some people it can even become a point of worship.

That often happens because our society portrays retirement as life's ultimate goal, or the holy grail achievement that ushers in the ideal or perfect phase of life. But that's just not the case, life's ultimate goal is getting into heaven and that's a message I don't want people to miss or realize too late.

As I began this journey and started looking for content around a Christian retirement, I didn't find much. I found a few articles and sermons but I felt something was missing and I didn't feel like references to silver crowns, old age and wisdom encapsulated everything that God created retirement to be.

Now don't get me wrong, we all work hard for our gray hairs and there's usually a lot of heartache and pain involved in the accumulation of wisdom, but I just felt this pull or tug to dig in and develop something with a fresh perspective, which is why I chose to focus on the four gospels of the New Testament for this series.

My hope for this retirement devotional is that it:

- Transforms your mindset from savings to salvation and ever-lasting life

- Breaks old and outdated thoughts feelings and ideas so you don't feel lost, alone or out of sorts

- That it positions you to use your spiritual gifts and talents for greater kingdom impact and legacy

- And that it helps to strengthen your relationship with the Lord through daily prayers

With that in mind I think Mark 8:22-25 is the ideal analogy for the start of this devotional. According to the Gospel, "*Jesus came to Bethsaida where a blind man begged to be healed. Jesus led the blind man out to the village, spit on his eyes and then put his hands on him. Then he asked, "Do you see anything?" and the man replied he could see but not clearly. Once more Jesus placed his hands on the man and his eyes were open and he could see clearly.*"

With this devotional I hope that God not only places his hands on you during your retirement journey, but that He also helps you see clearly the plans He has in place for you in retirement.

Just as Jesus could have healed the man the first-time, He placed his hands on the man, but instead, he revealed his new future gradually, so he could see God's work in progress.

So too, is the case for life in retirement. Everything may not be clear and easy to see or understand at first, but gradually and over time you will adapt, and adjust well if your focus is on the Lord and storing up treasures for Heaven.

The book was designed so that it could be used as a personal devotional as well as a four-week group study. In both cases, my goal was to illustrate that Jesus's ministry is just as relevant to every day life in retirement as it was for everyday life 2,000 years ago.

I hope it helps you to develop a God-centered plan that prepares you to ultimately hear the words, "Well done my good and faithful servant"

If you are interested in the eight companion videos, you can access them for free through Youtube.com (search retirement ministries) RetirementMinistries.com or with RightNowMedia.com. The videos serve as bookends for each week, meaning they are laid out to help you start and finish each week with a video. For example, the first video references week one day one in the book and the second video covers week one day five. This first day then fifth day order continues through each week and is detailed below.

Week One
Video 1: Day 1: Saving The Best For Last
Video 2: Day 5: Dark Side Of Retirement

Week Two
Video 3: Day 1: Retirement Focus
Video 4: Day 5: Faithful Friends

Week Three
Video 5: Day 1: Retirement Setback
Video 6: Day 5: Retirement Stones

Week Four
Video 7: Day 1: Retirement's Only Guarantee
Video 8: Bonus Day: First Place Retirement

Additionally, please visit RetirementMinistries.com to download our free *Retirement Prayers Guide,* which was created to pray a blessing over the mental, social, physical, spiritual, and financial aspects of your life in retirement.

Week 1

Romans 13:11
"And do this, understanding the present time: The hour has already come for you to wake up from your slumber, because our salvation is nearer now than when we first believed."

Saving The Best For Last

"When the master of ceremonies tasted the water that was now wine, not knowing where it had come from (though, of course, the servants knew), he called the bridegroom over. "A host always serves the best wine first," he said. "Then, when everyone has had a lot to drink, he brings out the less expensive wine. But you have saved the best until now!" John 2:9-10

Jesus had a profound way of changing things up. He altered ideas, norms, lives, and I believe in this example, also paved the way to get people thinking differently about the plans He has in store for them in retirement.

As the story around Jesus's first miracle unfolds, we are made aware that it was a common practice at weddings during this time to serve the best wine first and then bring out the lesser quality alcohol later, after guests were feeling lively and their senses were dulled.

In a similar way, society today places a bigger emphasis or higher value on youth, sending a message that a person's best and most productive years were the earlier ones… When they were in school or building their career.

But I think its important to point out, that's what society says, not what scripture implies. We know this because we are called to be a light, the salt of the earth, and vessel for change no matter our age or stage of life.

The reality is, retirement offers believers a profound opportunity to shift gears and remove much of the noise the outside or secular world can create while we are working.

In other words, retirement offers you the opportunity to hone-in and focus more intently on the plans God has for you during this next phase of life.

That means not holding anything back or serving in a lesser way. This is a time of life that can be filled with hope, personal growth, and transformation… making it the perfect time to change what other people think or believe about life or people in retirement by bringing out your best right now - and using it to expand His kingdom in fresh and exciting ways.

Daily Prayer:

"Lord help me understand the plans you have for me in retirement. Help me to use my gifts and talents to have an impact on your Kingdom, and to be a light to others by bringing out my best in retirement."

Questions For Reflection:

The idea of turning water into wine could be used as a metaphor for your own retirement by turning _____ into _____

_____

_____

_____

What have you built up or saved up that can be used to glorify God in ways that previously held you back while working?

_____

_____

_____

Support Scripture:

Philippians 3:14 "I press on to reach the end of the race and receive the heavenly prize for which God, through Christ Jesus, is calling us."

Retirement Fertilizer

"Then Jesus told this story: "A man planted a fig tree in his garden and came again and again to see if there was any fruit on it, but he was always disappointed. Finally, he said to his gardener, 'I've waited three years, and there hasn't been a single fig! Cut it down. It's just taking up space in the garden.' "The gardener answered, 'Sir, give it one more chance. Leave it another year, and I'll give it special attention and plenty of fertilizer. If we get figs next year, fine. If not, then you can cut it down.'" Luke 13:6-9

When it comes to creating a lush lawn or bountiful garden, one of the most important components is fertilizer. It serves as a crucial ingredient because trees, flowers, vegetables and shrubs can't produce everything they need to flourish on their own. They need outside forces, including a variety of nutrients to grow, heal and flourish.

In a similar fashion, we end up transplanted in retirement without any fertilizer. Many people assume their life will be fertile after they stop working simply because they reach a certain age or have enough money.

But the soil around them, in terms of relationships, health, identity and purpose, may not be ready for them to fully blossom. This can inevitably cause them to wilt or yield less during their initial transition.

5

This is important to point out because everything can initially seem okay when you first make the retirement transition. After all, when flowers are cut and placed in a vase, they can look healthy and even continue to bloom for a short period of time.

But they don't stay strong or come back fully year after year if they are not firmly rooted in a strong and secure way. True growth in retirement takes place over time and requires us to develop new habits and routines that reflect our spiritual beliefs and values.

Therefore, as you enter retirement, it's more important than ever to not only assess the soil around you but to also dig down and take a look at your roots because the key ingredient to bearing fruit in retirement is a strong relationship with our Lord and Savior Jesus Christ.

He is the light and living water, or divine source that will help you grow, heal, and flourish in retirement.

Daily Prayer:

"Lord I want to be rooted in You and use Your word as fertilizer to guide my daily life and impact others throughout retirement."

Questions For Reflection:

What is at the root of your faith? If you had to tell someone why you are a believer, what events or situations would you share?

_____

_____

_____

What regular routines or practices can you create in retirement to fertilize your own faith and that of those around you?

_____

_____

_____

Support Scripture:

John 4:10 "Jesus answered her, 'If you knew the gift of God and who it is that asks you for a drink, you would have asked him and he would have given you living water.'"

Retirement Decisions

"This is how Jesus the Messiah was born. His mother, Mary, was engaged to be married to Joseph. But before the marriage took place, while she was still a virgin, she became pregnant through the power of the Holy Spirit. Joseph, to whom she was engaged, was a righteous man and did not want to disgrace her publicly, so he decided to break the engagement quietly. As he considered this, an angel of the Lord appeared to him in a dream. "Joseph, son of David," the angel said, "do not be afraid to take Mary as your wife. For the child within her was conceived by the Holy Spirit. And she will have a son, and you are to name him Jesus for he will save his people from their sins." Matthew 1:18-21

Joseph faced a difficult decision. As he struggled to make sense of his situation, he felt the best-case scenario was to quietly drift away and leave Mary. But God had other plans in mind for him. He not only showed Joseph another option, but also gave him the courage to follow this calling.

Making a retirement decision can also feel daunting. There are a lot of *"What-if"* and *"What-now"* questions to consider, not to mention a variety of social pressures that come with reaching a traditional retirement age.

In some cases, it can even feel like you have no option or choice but to retire because of a company closing, health condition, or need to support family.

Many people have no idea that retirement is one of the top 10 most stressful life events and that 20 of the other 43 items on that same list can take place during retirement. In other words, it's a minefield of change that can cause some people to feel overwhelmed and out of sorts.

As a result, many people turn to financial professionals to help them try and sort everything out. But here's the reality! You will never have it all figured out for one simple reason.

God wants you to rely on Him for direction and support. Our God is a God of new beginnings, therefore don't go into a retirement decision assuming it's best to break off your engagement with work and drift away! Consider it a rebirth filled with the power of the Holy Spirit!

Daily Prayer:

"Lord, please help me make the most of this transition and to help me fulfill and see your long-term plans for me and Your Kingdom."

Questions For Reflection:

What situations have you been in before that caused you to rely on God for direction? What did you learn from it?

_____

_____

_____

What is one thing people would be surprised to learn that you are doing or trying in retirement?

_____

_____

_____

Support Scripture:

Philippians 4:6-7 "Do not be anxious about anything, but in every situation, by prayer and petition, with thanksgiving, present your requests to God. And the peace of God, which transcends all understanding, will guard your hearts and your minds in Christ Jesus."

Retirement Role

"Afterward Jesus went up on a mountain and called out the ones he wanted to go with him. And they came to him. Then he appointed twelve of them and called them his apostles. They were to accompany him, and he would send them out to preach, giving them authority to cast out demons. These are the twelve he chose: Simon, James son of Zebedee and his brother John Andrew, Philip, Bartholomew, Matthew, Thomas, James son of Alphaeus, Thaddaeus, Simon the Zealot and Judas Iscariot, who betrayed him." Mark 3:13-19

Whenever we talk about the twelve disciples we do so with reverence and admiration because we know the whole story. We know the trials and tribulations they endured and had to overcome. However, in the very beginning, these folks were very common, no thrills type, everyday people.

In fact, in some Bible explanations, theologians note that when the calling of the disciples was recorded, very little information was provided because there wasn't much to talk about. They didn't have lengthy resumes, religious training, or an impressive list of accolades leading up to this time.

Prior to being called to follow Jesus, each of the disciples had a career. We know Matthew was a tax collector and that Andrew, Peter, James, and

John were fisherman. While the occupations of the other disciples may not have been known or recorded, Jesus called each of them away from their productive trade so they could pursue their spiritual trade.

Retirement can be framed in a similar fashion where God calls you away from focusing on your work to concentrating on His work. The inspiring aspect of this is that similar to the disciples, being a spiritual leader doesn't require years of seminary school or a special invitation from a religious organization.

It starts by having a heart and actions that reflect Jesus, which means being humble, gracious, forgiving, and loving as well as praying and serving others to name a few.

God calls and uses us all in some way. Therefore, no matter how big or small your personal calling may look or feel, be ready as 1 Peter 3:15 tells us "…Always be ready to tell everyone who asks you why you believe as you do. Be gentle as you speak and show respect."

Daily Prayer:

"Dear Lord, thank you for calling me to serve a special role in your Kingdom. Please guide me through Your word, wisdom and power to make all things happen."

Questions For Reflection:

What is or was your productive trade and what do you or did you like most about it?

_____

_____

_____

What skills and talents were you known for in your career / work life that can play a role in your spiritual trade?

_____

_____

_____

Support Scripture:

Luke 9:23-24 "And he said to all, 'If anyone would come after me, let him deny himself and take up his cross daily and follow me. For whoever would save his life will lose it, but whoever loses his life for my sake will save it.'"

Dark Side Of Retirement

"Then Jesus was led by the Spirit into the wilderness to be tempted there by the devil. For forty days and forty nights he fasted and became very hungry. During that time the devil came and said to him, "If you are the Son of God, tell these stones to become loaves of bread." Matthew 4:1-3

I would love to tell you that God is the only one who has plans for your retirement, but that's not the case. Major life changes like retirement can be an open door for the Devil to do his work. Satan loves to use change to disrupt your life.

In particular, the first few months or honeymoon phase can be the perfect time for Satan to set up camp. He wants you to do nothing, to avoid former co-workers, put that new exercise routine on hold, and watch more TV.

Yes, it may feel good for the first week or two and that's not to say, you don't deserve a little R&R after 30-40 years of work or some time to process your thoughts and emotions about this transition.

However, don't let Satan slip in and create some division between you and God with your idle mind and hands (see Proverbs 6:27) in terms of alcohol, isolation, and depression.

Research suggest that alcohol is the most used drug among older adults, with 64% of people 65 and older reporting high-risk drinking. Additionally, 25% of all seniors aged 60 and above report feeling isolated and lonely, and 43% can go days without talking to others and spend most of their time alone.

Moreover, retired people are twice as likely to report feeling symptoms of depression than those who were still working. The likelihood of suffering from clinical depression actually goes up by about 40% after retiring.

It's a dark side of retirement that isn't usually talked about or planned for. Which is why its also worth pointing out that Jesus wasn't tempted inside the temple or at Baptism, he was tempted when he was tired, hungry, thirsty, and alone, or when he was most vulnerable. The devil will use the same approach with us because he is constantly looking for an entry point and retirement can be an easy one.

Daily Prayer:

"Heavenly Father, help keep me aware and alert to Satan's many temptations and allow me to use your word as a sword in spiritual battles."

Questions For Reflection:

What temptations could play a role in derailing your kingdom impact during retirement?

_____

_____

_____

After reading the support scripture below, how will you use the Armor of God and specifically the Shield of Faith to "extinguish all the arrows of the evil one?"

_____

_____

_____

Support Scripture:

Ephesians 6:13-18 "Therefore, put on every piece of God's armor so you will be able to resist the enemy in the time of evil. Then after the battle you will still be standing firm. Stand your ground, putting on the belt of truth and the body armor of God's righteousness. For shoes, put on the peace that comes from the Good News so that you will be fully prepared. In addition to all of these, hold up the shield of faith to stop the fiery arrows of the devil. Put on salvation as your helmet, and take the sword of the Spirit, which is the word of God. Pray in the Spirit at all times and on every occasion. Stay alert and be persistent in your prayers for all believers everywhere."

Week 1: Summary & Reflection

In week one we covered several important retirement concepts including the idea that this can be your best phase of life, how we need to dig down to see what you are rooted in, and how we can use the Lord as fertilizer for growth in retirement.

We also discussed, how retirement itself can be a difficult decision that we need to trust God with, that we are being called to leave our productive trade for our spiritual trade and finally, how the Devil can have retirement plans for you too.

Personal Application:

Retirement is a major transformation, and many people approach it with this big idea that their new life in retirement will completely transform them into something new and different.

Which sounds good on the surface until you start trying to do it. When was the last time you changed your daily routine after 30 or 40 years of repeated activity… or made a significant shift in who you see and talk to on a daily basis, where you live, how you stay mentally and physically active or relevant?

Change is hard and most people avoid it rather than seek it out. So let me help you shift your perspective on turning your life in retirement from water to wine. Michelangelo's approach to carving a masterpiece out of marble centers was rooted in a belief that God had already created the statue within the marble, and it was his job to get rid of the excess.

Think about that. Our true selves are waiting behind these hard, outside layers of stone that have been put around us. Things like our work environment, negative people and situations, demands from others, and even technology.

Let's not forget that there are also a series of layers that the media and other people put up around the concept of retirement.

We are constantly bombarded by mainstream images of what a perfect retirement is supposed to look and feel like, but most of it has very little to do with what God originally designed in you.

Therefore, think about some things that need to be chiseled away. Some areas of excess that can be refined and reshaped.

Then turn these things over to Master of the Ceremony and follow his word and promises to transform your life and quench your thirst for peace, grace, and eternal life.

Personal Thoughts & Notes:

Week 2

John 2:17
"The world and its desires pass away, but whoever does the will of God lives forever."

Retirement Focus

"As Jesus and the disciples continued on their way to Jerusalem, they came to a certain village where a woman named Martha welcomed him into her home. Her sister, Mary, sat at the Lord's feet, listening to what he taught. But Martha was distracted by the big dinner she was preparing. She came to Jesus and said, "Lord, doesn't it seem unfair to you that my sister just sits here while I do all the work? Tell her to come and help me." But the Lord said to her, "My dear Martha, you are worried and upset over all these details! There is only one thing worth being concerned about. Mary has discovered it, and it will not be taken away from her." Luke 10:38-42

I don't know if there is a better illustration that highlights a major flaw as to how people approach life leading up to retirement.

Just as Martha's desire to serve got in the way of neglecting the most important person she would ever come into contact with, people can make the same mistake by focusing so much on getting ready for the financial side of retirement that they neglect the most important things they will need during it.

They work extra hours, save, sacrifice, miss family functions, are too tired to hit the gym and sometimes put their marriage and other relationships on the backburner. Hoping that once they finally reach retirement that they will be able to restore it. But that's not how it always works.

Just because you suddenly have time to devote to those things now, doesn't mean that those around you will have the time or desire to reciprocate.

The big question here isn't whether you are going to be like Mary or Martha but rather understanding that you need to find balance between listening and laboring and giving priority to your walk with God.

Daily Prayer:

"Almighty Father, please help me avoid neglecting important things and strike a better balance with the many people, places, and things you have put into my life. I don't want to miss any opportunity with you Lord!"

Questions For Reflection:

What areas of your life have you neglected or put on hold in your effort to reach retirement?

_____

_____

_____

How might your definition of finding balance in life differ from Jesus's view and what opportunities for immediate change are in front of you right now?

_____

_____

_____

Support Scripture:

James 5:16 "So confess your sins to one another. Pray for one another so that you might be healed. The prayer of a godly person is powerful. Things happen because of it."

Retirement Sin

"Simon, Simon, Satan has asked to sift each of you like wheat. But I have pleaded in prayer for you, Simon, that your faith should not fail. So when you have repented and turned to me again, strengthen your brothers." Peter said, "Lord, I am ready to go to prison with you, and even to die with you." But Jesus said, "Peter, let me tell you something. Before the rooster crows tomorrow morning, you will deny three times that you even know me." Luke 22:31-34

Let's face it, we all have breaking points and are far from perfect. We know that Peter did in fact fail his friend and Lord three times despite saying he wouldn't. He had the best of intentions but fell short.

Likewise, it's very likely we may not only fail the Lord but in some circumstances either deny knowing Him or avoid inviting Him into certain aspects of our life. That's not the plan or goal, which is why its so important to understand what to do when it happens.

You may be entering retirement with the best of intentions or may already be retired. It may not happen right away but at some point, you may find yourself isolating from family or friends, avoiding small group or the fellowship of church, not sharing your special gifts or talents, or not giving your mental of physical health the attention it needs. Some people may even turn to drugs or alcohol to cope.

The reality is, we are all sinners and will fail the Lord by yielding to some temptation or sin. When that happens, we must turn back to Jesus and repent, as well as find ways to turn the mess into a message that strengthens others.

As we know, Jesus not only forgave Peter, but also used him as a cornerstone for the church. The Rooster's crow in this verse serves as a symbol of Peter's denial and repentance, as well as that of his restoration. Only God can take the shattered pieces of our life and glue them back together stronger than before.

No matter what may be broken in your life leading up to or already in retirement, each day is a new day with the Lord and an opportunity to turn, repent, and be restored.

Daily Prayer:

"Lord Jesus, I come to you a sinner who has fallen short, please forgive me for my sins and help me to make changes so that I may glorify you and live out the purpose you have created for me."

Questions For Reflection:

In the past, what steps did you take to rectify a situation where you fell short and how did the situation strengthen you?

_____

_____

_____

What word, phrase, or verse can you use as a warning or rosters crow, to help you avoid temptation and sin in retirement?

_____

_____

_____

Support Scripture:

Matthew 6:13 "And lead us not into temptation, but deliver us from the evil one."

Career Versus Calling

"As Jesus was walking along, he saw a man named Matthew sitting at his tax collector's booth. "Follow me and be my disciple," Jesus said to him. So Matthew got up and followed him. Later, Matthew invited Jesus and his disciples to his home as dinner guests, along with many tax collectors and other disreputable sinners. But when the Pharisees saw this, they asked his disciples, "Why does your teacher eat with such scum?" When Jesus heard this, he said, "Healthy people don't need a doctor—sick people do." Then he added, "Now go and learn the meaning of this Scripture: 'I want you to show mercy, not offer sacrifices.' For I have come to call not those who think they are righteous, but those who know they are sinners." Matthew 9:9-13

There is a major difference between a career and your calling. In other words, work is what you do, not who you are.

That's easier said than done for some people because they have invested a lot of time and energy into their work life. But the reality is, no matter how much you love your work, it can't love you back.

That's a powerful statement to understand because as you make your way out of the workforce you will need to focus on things that can love you back.

27

Which is why it's so important to take the time to look beyond your career and to find God's calling for you, because God not only created you, He did so with a purpose and special mission for you.

Scripture teaches that every Christian is given spiritual gifts at the time of their salvation and is gifted to serve as part of Christ's body…to be the hands and feet of Jesus. But it doesn't stop there because we all have natural talents and abilities that God gave us at birth as well.

That doesn't mean you have to say "Yes" to every request or volunteer for every committee or mission trip. Instead, see it as an opportunity to be more intentional with what you have been given, and to use those things to shape other people's lives while giving yourself purpose in retirement.

Daily Prayer:

"Heavenly Father, thank you for blessing me with special gifts and talents. Please show me how I can use them to foster joy, love, and compassion in others and thereby allow them to get to know and love you."

Questions For Reflection:

What is your personal ministry or way you feel
called to serve and have an impact on certain
people, places, or situations?

_____

_____

_____

What is your most inspiring example of someone
you have seen living out their mission and using
their gifts, talents, and abilities for maximum
kingdom impact?

_____

_____

_____

Support Scripture:

_Peter 4:10 "Each of you should use whatever gift
you have received to serve others, as faithful
stewards of God's grace in its various forms."_

Solid Foundation

"Anyone who listens to my teaching and follows it is wise, like a person who builds a house on solid rock. Though the rain comes in torrents and the floodwaters rise and the winds beat against that house, it won't collapse because it is built on bedrock. But anyone who hears my teaching and doesn't obey it is foolish, like a person who builds a house on sand. When the rains and floods come and the winds beat against that house, it will collapse with a mighty crash." Matthew 7:24-27

While retirement brochures and commercials won't say it, you will inevitably face storms and heavy torrents throughout retirement. You will have to make difficult decisions and choices, some of which may feel like there is no "good" or "right" answer.

In these situations, fear, anxiety, and uncertainty can creep in and take root. All things that can paralyze, weaken and distract you from the things you need to be doing.

During these uncertain times, one of the best things to do is to turn to the things that are certain, meaning Jesus Christ. He is the only sure thing we have and the only one to overcome life's ultimate fear and consequence: Death.

His teachings provide us the foundation for which to make all decisions and to overcome any situation. The power of His parables is that they contain several layers of meaning which can be understood on different levels depending on each individual person or situation.

It's one reason why we hear people say they have read the same verse or passage many times yet continue to walk away with something different and useful each time.

Reality is, a meaningful life in retirement won't be one without problems, but rather one in which you learn to overcome them. Therefore, consider the teachings of Christ like a seed that has the ability to bring out new, more abundant life each time you enter into it. Use it as the foundation for your retirement decision and life.

Daily Prayer:

"God, thank you for being my rock and foundation, please help me to stand strong when storms come and to help others avoid building their retirement on the shifting sands of money and other earthly possessions."

Questions For Reflection:

What are some ways you have witnessed others build a life in retirement on sand?

_____

_____

_____

If someone had to write a sermon about your life in retirement, what are three things you would want them to say about you?

_____

_____

_____

Support Scripture:

1 Corinthians 3:11 "For no one can lay a foundation other than that which is already laid, which is Jesus Christ."

Faithful Friends

"Some men came carrying a paralyzed man on a sleeping mat. They tried to take him inside to Jesus, but they couldn't reach him because of the crowd. So they went up to the roof and took off some tiles. Then they lowered the sick man on his mat down into the crowd, right in front of Jesus."
Luke 5:18-19

Wow! What a group of friends. They not only went out of their way to bring this man to see Jesus but were so persistent that they opted to dig down through multiple layers of roofing to make sure Jesus could heal their friend.

Interestingly, it wasn't just the paralytics faith that impressed Jesus but rather the faith of his friends. For better or worse, our faith affects others, and while we can't make other people Christians, we can show them the light through our words, actions, and love.

Fact is, God created us as social beings, so we need human connections for physical, emotional, and spiritual health. God wants us to connect with others on an intimate level and grow together but here's the thing, many pre-retirees are never told that once they are retired, the luxury of running into and connecting with people they know can suddenly and dramatically decrease.

Therefore, it may not come as a surprise that one of the biggest factors to making a successful transition from work-life to home-life is your social network, or who you chose to surround yourself with.

Developing and strengthening your social network takes time and effort. That may mean joining a small group, volunteering for more than one organization, participating in an exercise class or mission-based activity.

In any event, seek to build relationships like the paralyzed man that can not only bring you closer to God but also give you people to rely on and turn to during difficult times.

Daily Prayer:

"Lord God, thank you for the people you have put into my life and those still to come. Allow me to not only be a friend like those who brought a paralyzed man to be healed by Your son Jesus but to also have friends like them in my corner as well."

Questions For Reflection:

What are three key things for building and maintaining strong and meaningful friendships?

_____

_____

_____

How can you use your faith to carry others toward a personal relationship with Christ?

_____

_____

_____

Support Scripture:

1 Thessalonians 5:11 "And so encourage one another and help one another, just as you are now doing."

Week 2: Summary & Reflection

In week two we covered several important retirement ideas including how being busy and consumed by worry can take away what God has in store for your life in retirement. The fact that we all fall short but are given a fresh start through repentance, and the need to build our retirement foundations on God's word and promises.

Additionally, we talked about the need to use the gifts and talents we have been giving for Kingdom impact, and how God has a plan to use us all in some meaningful way and the benefit of surrounding ourselves with faithful friends.

Personal Application:

The role that God can play in a person's retirement is interesting because so often traditional retirement plans are often designed to get people from point A to point B.

However, as you begin to sketch out this seemingly straightforward journey, it's easy to forget that, like the early apostles, there are sections of every journey that are uncharted, with boundaries outside of what can be seen, explained, or anticipated.

It's common, especially for people today, to overlook these voids and simply assume that their life and plans will remain within the mapped area.

But that's a secular view of life after work, where the unknown is out of the picture and off limits. Which is why I want to encourage you to embrace and explore these uncharted areas with the God of possibilities.

In other words, to walk off the path in order to survey the depths of your heart and soul, seeking out those distant places, and expanding the retirement horizon instead of putting boundaries around it.

Approaching retirement as a voyage that embraces both the known and the unknown leads to very different conversations and results.

Retirement doesn't need to be a strange place where we end up, full of excuses as to why so much of life ended up in the background, out of sight and off the map.

Instead start to infuse your life with a biblical focus and commitment - because great personal stories and family legacies aren't created by following the same plan as everyone else.

Instead, they are blazed by going where there is no path and leaving a trail for others to follow.

Personal Thoughts & Notes:

Week 3

Retirement Setbacks

"On hearing it, many of his disciples said, "This is a hard teaching. Who can accept it?" Aware that his disciples were grumbling about this, Jesus said to them, "Does this offend you? Then what if you see the Son of Man ascend to where he was before! The Spirit gives life; the flesh counts for nothing. The words I have spoken to you—they are full of the Spirit and life. Yet there are some of you who do not believe." For Jesus had known from the beginning which of them did not believe and who would betray him. He went on to say, "This is why I told you that no one can come to me unless the Father has enabled them." From this time many of his disciples turned back and no longer followed him." John 6: 60-71

I don't think I have ever heard someone say, "My favorite scripture is where a large group of people pick up and leave Jesus for an easier way of life."

While it may not be popular sermon material, it highlights the fact that a believer's journey to and through retirement will come with both ups and downs.

At different points in our lives, we may be tempted to turn away because Jesus' lessons can be difficult. Frustration, doubt, or confusion are just a few of the things people can feel as they navigate the new waters of retirement.

Which begs the question, when these things happen will our response be to give up, ignore certain teachings, or reject Christ?

While many believers may not completely turn away from God, in new or unfamiliar situations, we may opt to compartmentalize Him.

Meaning, we give Him our time and attention on Sunday at church or during small group but exclude him from other areas of our lives, particularly in areas we struggle.

Therefore, memorize some scripture or have a prayer ready in a journal that you can turn to when you face a hard teaching. Embrace it rather than reject it.

Daily Prayer:

"Lord God, Father, I want you to be present in every aspect of my life, not just the areas I choose. During difficult times, please help me better understand what the teachings mean and how it applies to my life and those around me."

Questions For Reflection:

What life events or situations may have caused some doubt or tested your faith in the past? How did you overcome or work through it?

_____
_____
_____

What is one area of your life where you don't involve or turn to Jesus enough?

_____
_____
_____

Support Scripture:

Matthew 7:13-14 "Enter by the narrow gate. For the gate is wide and the way is easy that leads to destruction, and those who enter by it are many. For the gate is narrow and the way is hard that leads to life, and those who find it are few."

Family Challenges

"After this, Jesus traveled around Galilee. He wanted to stay out of Judea, where the Jewish leaders were plotting his death. But soon it was time for the Jewish Festival of Shelters, and Jesus' brothers said to him, "Leave here and go to Judea, where your followers can see your miracles! You can't become famous if you hide like this! If you can do such wonderful things, show yourself to the world!" For even his brothers didn't believe in him."
John 7:1-5

As if losing some followers wasn't bad enough, Jesus returns to his hometown and even his family doubts Him. They ask Him to leave and sarcastically tell Him to go put on a show for everyone at the festival.

Reality is, not everyone is a believer. They simply can't get past certain things because they can't see it, explain it or comprehend it. As a result, this causes some people to get cynical about Christian life. Which can be even more challenging when its close family and friends who are drifting from their faith or putting themselves ahead of God.

Like other stages and phases of life, family dynamics can get tricky in retirement. The best laid plans to visit family, spend time with the grand kids or even help an aging parent can quickly get complicated, at times causing people to feel unwelcome or unwanted.

Whether kids move to switch jobs, a family rift causes a divide, or health factors limit your ability to travel and engage with family, there will likely be family let-downs at some point.

But the story of Jesus' brothers can actually give us hope for our loved ones. During the early stages of Jesus' ministry, it must have appeared very unlikely that they would ever become his disciples. However, we know they not only came around as believers but also leaders and martyrs in the church.

Make praying for your loved ones a regular part of your retirement life and seek new ways to connect with them and show them your heart for Jesus.

Daily Prayer:

"Lord when family issues arise, please help me understand it's only temporary and that I can always rely on you for love, grace and support. Guide me in being your hands and feet and bringing my family to a relationship with you Lord."

Questions For Reflection:

Which family members and friends would you like to see come to faith?

_____

_____

_____

What family let-downs have you experienced and what did you learn from them?

_____

_____

_____

Support Scripture:

Romans 10:19 "Because, if you confess with your mouth that Jesus is Lord and believe in your heart that God raised him from the dead, you will be saved."

Flavor Of Life

"You are the salt of the earth. But what good is salt if it has lost its flavor? Can you make it salty again? It will be thrown out and trampled underfoot as worthless. "You are the light of the world—like a city on a hilltop that cannot be hidden. No one lights a lamp and then puts it under a basket. Instead, a lamp is placed on a stand, where it gives light to everyone in the house. In the same way, let your good deeds shine out for all to see, so that everyone will praise your heavenly Father."
Matthew 5:13-16

One of the challenges new and existing retirees have as they make the transition from work life to home life is replacing their work identity and filling their time.

These two factors are not usually part of the traditional retirement planning process and can take some time for people to figure out on their own.

But here, Jesus provides divine purpose and direction for all Christians. We have a job or role to be the salt of the earth and preserve God's place, promises, and ways. We are also told to be beacons of light, or bright and shiny objects in our dark and chaotic world.

Fact is, the Bible doesn't endorse the way many people perceive retirement. Nowhere does scripture offer ideas or suggestions for living a leisure filled, do whatever you want, whenever you want lifestyle. With this scripture, it tells us specifically who we are and what we are to do.

Therefore, in this new phase of life, there is a need to develop new routines and practices in order to make a difference in the flavor of the world and to shine a light toward heaven and the way to eternal life.

Use this empowering message as a reminder to wake up every day with a renewed sense of divine purpose, direction, and commitment.

Daily Prayer:

"Savior, thank you for giving my life flavor. Please help me take steps to preserve your ways and truths in retirement and to help me give others a taste of a better, eternal life that shines for you Lord."

Questions For Reflection:

What would your life in retirement look and feel like if it lost its flavor?

_____

_____

_____

What are three things that excite you, inspire you, or cause you to "light up" that can serve as a beacon of hope and faith for others?

_____

_____

_____

Support Scripture:

Hebrews 13:16 "Don't forget to do good and to share what you have because God is pleased with these kinds of sacrifices."

Retirement Glory

"The next day the large crowd that had come to the feast heard that Jesus was coming to Jerusalem. So they took branches of palm trees and went out to meet him, crying out, 'Hosanna! Blessed is he who comes in the name of the Lord, even the King of Israel!'" John 12:12-13

You have likely seen this passage portrayed in a movie or experienced a reenactment of it during a Palm Sunday service where Jesus is welcomed into Jerusalem with much adoration, praise, and fanfare. People throughout the city are waving palms and shouting "Hosana" as the new King comes into town to usher in a new era of life and prosperity for Jerusalem.

In a similar way, retirement acts like a lifelong goal fulfilled. It comes at us with much hype and fanfare. People celebrate leaving the workplace and the idea that a new, more fulfilling era is upon them. But just as Jesus was praised one moment, the tide quickly changed just days later when the very people who celebrated Him, turned against Him.

Thankfully, we don't face crucifixion at the end of our careers, but people, places, and things can change very quickly in retirement. Many pre-retirees create unrealistic expectations about how different and fulfilling it's going to be only to learn that on their own, their thoughts and desires don't exactly measure up.

The reality is, retirement is empty! There is nothing there so you have to fill it up with things that are important to you, otherwise, other things including Satan can find their way in it and derail the best laid plans. Furthermore, during the transition, you lose more than you gain. Yes, you gain time and freedom, but you also lose routine, identity, purpose, connection and mental stimulus to name a few. Fact of the matter is, money, time and constant leisure have very little to do with true freedom which only God can provide.

True freedom is void of fear, shame, guilt, and worry. It's knowing you're loved for who you are, and loving others for what and where they are in life. It's an opportunity to genuinely be who you are and to live the life God created for you.

Therefore, don't get caught up in the hype and assume retirement will be this ideal phase of life where everything automatically works out. Start filing it up with things that will glorify God.

Daily Prayer:

"Almighty Father, please help me see beyond the earthly glory of reaching retirement and deal with the many changes that come with it. Please help me to rely on you and see this time of life from Your point of view rather than my own."

Questions For Reflection:

What's all the hype about getting to retirement? What are some of the factors that people are looking forward to that can end up turning on them?

_____

_____

_____

What kind of freedom does a relationship with Christ offer?

_____

_____

_____

Support Scripture:

2 Corinthians 3:17 "Now the Lord is the Spirit, and where the Spirit of the Lord is, there is freedom."

Removing Stones

"So they rolled the stone aside. Then Jesus looked up to heaven and said, "Father, thank you for hearing me. You always hear me, but I said it out loud for the sake of all these people standing here, so that they will believe you sent me." Then Jesus shouted, "Lazarus, come out!" And the dead man came out, his hands and feet bound in graveclothes, his face wrapped in a headcloth. Jesus told them, "Unwrap him and let him go!" John 11:41-44

In a popular quote, a wise person suggests that the graveyard is one of the richest place on earth because it contains so many hopes and dreams that were never fulfilled simply because someone was too afraid to take that first step.

The concept of retirement can also be portrayed as a time of life where hopes, dreams, relationships, health, and other things go to die. It can leave people with no other purpose or passion, struggling to adapt and wondering why it doesn't look or feel right. It can be a heartbreaking reality if we dwell on it and don't find creative ways to avoid it.

Putting this verse into perspective, we all have some sort of tombstone that is blocking our way, our future, and our callings.

It can feel like a massive weight you can't move and as a result, cause some people to give up and put "grave clothes" on their goals, hopes, and dreams before it's time to.

So, I want to encourage you to never doubt what the Lord can do for and through you when you have faith. Therefore, develop and use that faith to resurrect any hopes and dreams that may have been on hold.

Daily Prayer:

"Lord God, I come to you in faith and ask that you remove anything that is blocking me from fulfilling the plans you have for me. Please help restore any lost hope, dreams, or plans and help me do so by aligning them with You Lord, so I can fulfill my calling here on earth."

Questions For Reflection:

What is one thing that has been blocking your way toward a deeper or specific calling?

_____

_____

_____

What are two important life pursuits that you would like to resurrect in retirement?

_____

_____

_____

Support Scripture:

Philippians 4:13 "For I can do everything through Christ, who gives me strength."

Week 3: Summary & Reflection

In week three we covered several important retirement ideas including the fact that Jesus's teaching can come with some hard lessons that may cause some people to stray, including family challenges with our closest loved ones

Additionally, we referenced the need to not only keep but share our spiritual flavor, discussed how retirement can be perceived as the ultimate life goal, and lastly, that we all have stones blocking our path and we need to call on the Lord to remove them.

Personal Application:

As many of you know, there is a longstanding belief that people have right-brain or left-brain tendencies, inclinations, or personality traits that cause them to act and think a certain way based on the more dominant hemispheres of their brains.

So-called left-brained people are described as logical, analytical and detail-oriented. They tend to be objective and fact-oriented, so they are good at math, engineering and other jobs and careers requiring fact-based thinking.

Right-brained people, on the other hand, are thought to be creative, perceptive and intuitive freethinkers. Their perspectives and approaches are more subjective and expressive, so they're associated with creative jobs and careers.

All very interesting information, but it's simply not true. The right brain/left brain idea is a myth rooted in old and outdated information. What research actually proves is that even though different sides of the brain are responsible for different tasks, we use both sides equally, meaning logic and creativity are not separate or exclusive.

In a similar way, when it comes to retirement, we have been conditioned to believe that by hitting a certain age and having a specific amount of money saved will ensure a happy retirement. However, as the idea of retirement evolves with more and more people reaching it, we are quickly learning that is simply not true.

Money and hitting a certain age has very little to do with ones happiness in retirement. It's the complete person, inclusive of the spiritual, social, physical and mental aspects of it that help foster a successful transition.

When you start to view your retirement in its entirety, you can start to see more of Gods work within your life.

You can also see Him move in area's you didn't realize needed your attention. It's why daily communication with God through prayer is key to making the most of your years in it.

Personal Thoughts & Notes:

Week 4

Mark 13:32-33
"But about that day or hour no one knows, not even the angels in heaven, nor the Son, but only the Father. Be on guard! Be alert! You do not know when that time will come."

Retirement's Only Guarantee

"Don't let your hearts be troubled. Trust in God, and trust also in me. There is more than enough room in my Father's home. If this were not so, would I have told you that I am going to prepare a place for you? When everything is ready, I will come and get you, so that you will always be with me where I am. "And you know the way to where I am going." "No, we don't know, Lord," Thomas said. "We have no idea where you are going, so how can we know the way?" Jesus told him, "I am the way, the truth, and the life. No one can come to the Father except through me. If you had really known me, you would know who my Father is. From now on, you do know him and have seen him!" John 14:1-7

Many people wrongly assume that when they retire, they have 20-30 years to do what they want, whenever they want.

But that is just not the case because the only earthly guarantee that comes with retirement is that at some point, you will die. You could be called home the very first day of your retirement or well past your 100th birthday.

In any event, questions about our own mortality or ability to enjoy retirement seem like the ideal conversations to avoid … and most people do.

However, I want to encourage you to use those conversations as motivating factors. To give your retirement more meaning by approaching it as if every day could be your last. By focusing on the here and now, you can get your arms around the essential things that will impact your eternal life rather than your earthly one.

Thankfully, Jesus has secured an eternal life for you and we can look forward to it because He promised that to us, and that He would come back. Jesus is the way because He is both part God and man, and once we unite our lives with Him we are uniting our lives with God.

Daily Prayer:

"Dear God, thank you for preparing a place for me and showing me the way to everlasting life and love. Please guide me in managing my daily life so that I may glorify your divine kingdom with the time you have given me here on earth."

Questions For Reflection:

What three pieces of wisdom do you think are essential to pass on to get the next steward ready?

_____

_____

_____

When you are called home, who are you looking forward to being reunited with in Heaven?

_____

_____

_____

Support Scripture:

2 Timothy 1:14 "You have had something very important entrusted to you; make sure you look after it, through the holy spirit who dwells in us."

Stewardship In Retirement

"In the beginning was the Word, and the Word was with God, and the Word was God. He was with God in the beginning. Through him all things were made; without him nothing was made that has been made. In him was life, and that life was the light of all mankind. The light shines in the darkness, and the darkness has not overcome it".
John 1:1-5

Let me quickly then explain one of the most important foundational truths about retirement: "It's all God's anyway!" Through Him all things were made. When God created, He made something out of nothing, and you only exist because God created you.

That means, your life, investments, house, car, family, friends, health and more all belong to him. They are on loan and it's your job is to care for them, no matter how big or small, to the best of your ability. That's why you need to develop a stewardship mentality around everything in your retirement.

When you position yourself as a steward instead of an owner, you can approach topics that give many people stress and anxiety with less emotion and more discipline and action.

Worry wears people down and takes up valuable space in your heart and mind. In other words, over stressing about whether the stock market is going to crash, whether a change in political leadership will cause havoc, or how you are going to afford an increase in taxes or health care costs isn't going to stop or change it.

But you can be prepared for it by knowing who to turn to and using this stewardship mentality to avoid a lot of the procrastination and analysis paralysis that robs people from truly seeing and doing what God has planned for them.

An important part of retirement is also making sure the next stewards are ready. Not just by preparing and estate plan to transition wealth, but rather by transferring wisdom. After all, wealth doesn't create wisdom, but wisdom can both maintain as well as create wealth that goes beyond just the dollars and cents of life.

Daily Prayer:

"Lord I love and trust you with everything. Please make me a good steward of what you have loaned me so that I may make the most of it to expand your kingdom by turning my stress and worry into prayer."

Questions For Reflection:

What areas of your life are easiest to forget that God owns it and your role as a steward?   Your body, mind, heart, possessions, money, etc?

_____

_____

_____

What are a couple of retirement things you are procrastinating on or over analyzing?

_____

_____

_____

Support Scripture:

Colossians 1:16 "For by him all things were created, in heaven and on earth, visible and invisible, whether thrones or dominions or rulers or authorities—all things were created through him and for him."

Patched-up Retirement

"He told them this parable: "No one tears a piece out of a new garment to patch an old one. Otherwise, they will have torn the new garment, and the patch from the new will not match the old. And no one pours new wine into old wineskins. Otherwise, the new wine will burst the skins; the wine will run out and the wineskins will be ruined. No, new wine must be poured into new wineskins. And no one after drinking old wine wants the new, for they say, 'The old is better.'"
Luke 5:36-39

Wineskins were made from goat skins sewed together to form a tight water seal. Since new wine expands as it ages, it had to be put in a flexible or pliable wineskin. A used skin become rigid over time, so adding new wine would cause it to burst and spill.

Like old wineskins, the Pharisees were too rigid to accept Jesus who could not be contained within their many rules and traditions. Jesus came to forgive our sins and reconcile us with God and used this description to explain that His purpose was to bring something new.

Life after work comes as a fresh start and it's crucial, we don't enter it rigid and inflexible to new things. Your life should not be so structured that you have no room for a fresh touch of the spirit, a new method, or new idea.

This mindset is crucial to staying relevant and connected in retirement.

Just because you did things a certain way in the past while you were working doesn't mean it will work the same way in retirement.

So don't go into it assuming you know the best or right way, or that you can just patch things up with your newfound time and freedom. Look for ways to stay flexible and open-minded.

Approach other people, groups, and generations with a spirit of curiosity, looking for ways to understand and learn from them rather than assuming the role of teacher.

Daily Prayer:

"Mighty High God, make me a vessel of your love and message. Help me to grow and appreciate others in new ways and avoid being too rigid and structured to receive your calling and direction for me."

Questions For Reflection:

What areas of your life may have become to rigid and act like old wineskin, holding back new growth or expansion?

_____

_____

_____

What are three things you appreciate about or can learn from younger generations?

_____

_____

_____

Support Scripture:

Ephesians 3.21 *"To Him be glory in the church by Christ Jesus to all generations, forever and ever. Amen."*

Calculated Retirement

"Jesus soon saw a huge crowd of people coming to look for him. Turning to Philip, he asked, "Where can we buy bread to feed all these people?" He was testing Philip, for he already knew what he was going to do. Philip replied, "Even if we worked for months, we wouldn't have enough money to feed them!" Then Andrew, Simon Peter's brother, spoke up. "There's a young boy here with five barley loaves and two fish. But what good is that with this huge crowd?" "Tell everyone to sit down," Jesus said. So they all sat down on the grassy slopes. Then Jesus took the loaves, gave thanks to God, and distributed them to the people. Afterward he did the same with the fish. And they all ate as much as they wanted. After everyone was full, Jesus told his disciples, "Now gather the leftovers, so that nothing is wasted." So they picked up the pieces and filled twelve baskets with scraps left by the people who had eaten from the five barley loaves." John 6:5-13

There are so many great layers to this passage. It starts with money. As soon as Jesus asked Phillip about buying bread, he quickly calculated how many man-hours of work it would take to feed all those people.

He saw the task as impossible because he approached it as if everything depended on money and his efforts. But Jesus' approach is different.

Jesus bypassed all human effort and did the impossible.

Many people do something similar when it comes to retirement. They start calculating numbers and running figures that on the surface can feel impossible or overwhelming to deal with. But that's not what God wants you to focus on when it comes to retirement.

God can shatter the pint-sized expectations of what His followers can do if they would learn to bring Him what they have already been given. "Little is much when God is in it."

Christians must never believe their resources are too little to serve God. God delights in taking a humble, unassuming person and using him or her for His glory.

Therefore, don't just calculate the resources you think you need for retirement, calculate the impact you can have by being kind and loving, generous with your time and talents, as well as, encouraging to the lost and broken hearted.

Daily Prayer:

"Dear Lord, I know what may seem impossible to me is nothing for you. Thank you for your provision over my life and legacy in You."

Questions For Reflection:

How much time have you spent planning for the financial side of retirement compared to the personal and spiritual side of it?

_____

_____

_____

What aspect or area of your life feels like there isn't enough?

_____

_____

_____

Support Scripture:

Galatians 5:1 "It is for freedom that Christ has set us free. Stand firm, then, and do not let yourselves be burdened again by a yoke of slavery."

Lost & Found

"Or suppose a woman has ten silver coins and loses one. Won't she light a lamp and sweep the entire house and search carefully until she finds it? And when she finds it, she will call in her friends and neighbors and say, 'Rejoice with me because I have found my lost coin.' In the same way, there is joy in the presence of God's angels when even one sinner repents." Luke 15:8-10

In this time, Palestinian women received 10 silver coins as a wedding gift which carried both monetary value as well as sentimental value. The coins were a symbol like a wedding ring, and so, if any were lost, it was very distressing.

Unfortunately, in the process of making your way to retirement things can get lost along the way as well. As a result, some people may find that they are missing something valuable and unsure of how to get it back.

That may be a close relationship with a spouse, purpose and direction in their life, an estranged relationship with a child or former close friends, your health and vibrancy, and even your relationship with God.

The good news is that each individual is precious to Him and He not only grieves over every loss, but also rejoices whenever one of his children is found and brought into the Kingdom.

In other words, God doesn't want nine of the ten coins, He wants all of them to be in His possession.

Similar to the mercy and grace God gives to us, when it comes to mending personal relationships or other things that can get lost or broken, it may mean you have to take the first step in the reconciliation process, which isn't always easy to do. So, ask the Lord to help shine a light on those first steps and solutions.

Daily Prayer:

"Heavenly Father, thank you for the grace and mercy you show me on a regular basis. Thank you for the people and relationships you have put into my life and please help me find and embrace the missing coins in my life."

Questions For Reflection:

What is something of value that you lost but found later? What thoughts and emotions did you experience when you both lost it and found it?

_____

_____

_____

Is there a personal relationship that needs mending? What would a first step for you look like?

_____

_____

_____

Support Scripture:

Colossians 3:13 "Bear with each other and forgive one another if any of you has a grievance against someone. Forgive as the Lord forgave you."

First Place Retirement

"Seek the Kingdom of God above all else, and live righteously, and he will give you everything you need. "So don't worry about tomorrow, for tomorrow will bring its own worries. Today's trouble is enough for today." Matthew 6:33-34

A big part of traditional retirement planning is focused on worry and anxiety. Worrying about running out of money, being a burden to others, not leaving an inheritance, getting sick or losing a loved one. These factors are used as sales tactics to push certain financial products and services. While those things can happen, we also know that planning and understanding is key to eliminating them.

Jesus tells us not to worry about those needs that God promises to supply. Worry can impact your health, consume your thoughts, and reduce your productivity, which can negatively affect the way you treat others and your relationship with God.

Jesus contrasted heavenly values with earthly values when he explained that our first loyalty should be those things that do not fade, cannot be stolen or used up, and never wear out. We should not be fascinated with our possessions, lest they possess us.

Planning for tomorrow is time well spent, while worrying about tomorrow is just time wasted.

Careful planning involves thinking ahead, planning some initial steps, and trusting in God's guidance along the way.

So, as we close out this devotional, let me ask you, when it comes to retirement, what do you think more about? God or money? Which one do you have a written, detailed plan for? Fact is, people, possessions, and other desires compete for priority and any of them can quickly become the most important if you don't actively choose to give God first place.

Daily Prayer:

"Almighty Father I know you are the creator and owner of all things. Please help me develop a retirement life and plan that places you first and above all else so that I may do your will."

Questions For Reflection:

What are your two biggest retirement worries and how are you handing them over to Jesus?

_____

_____

_____

What are your three highest priorities for your life in retirement and have you written a plan to help you live them out?

_____

_____

_____

Support Scripture:

Romans 14:12 "So then each of us will give an account of himself to God."

Week 4: Summary & Reflection

In our final week we covered several important retirement ideas including the need to be flexible in retirement, to stop calculating the cost of everything and trusting God instead.

We also discussed how God wants all those who are lost to come home, how we can fall short in sin but bounce back thanks to His Grace, and how we are just Stewards of what the Lord has given us and need to take steps to use it according to His will.

Personal Application:

The Titanic was considered unsinkable because of its size, speed and design. It was nearly 900 feet long and more than 100 feet high. It was said to be the world's fastest ship, capable of reaching speeds of 30 knots. At the time, it was the most expensive and luxurious ship ever assembled.

It cost an estimated $7.5 million in 1912 dollars, the equivalent of $180 million today and boasted 10 decks, and first-time features including a swimming pool, Turkish baths, squash courts and a gym.

It was also equipped with a double-plated bottom and sixteen watertight compartments on the hull of the ship with doors that would close if water entered them. This was designed to provide the utmost in security. The company who built the Titanic put undue faith in the design of watertight compartments that composed its hull.

The compartments were not sealed at the top, so if too many of them in the bow were breached, seawater would flow from one compartment to the next in the same way water fills an ice cube tray. The probability of that happening was extremely low, given its other design features.

However, during the evening of Sunday, April 14 the Titanic's starboard side violently scraped an iceberg. Ten minutes after midnight, the order for passengers to head for the lifeboats was given because six of those hull compartments were ripped open and flooded immediately.

Unfortunately, the ship's design could only withstand four compartments flooding. At 2:20 a.m., the Titanic finally sank. Breaking in half, as it plunged downward to the sea floor.

On paper, it was the place to be and people aspired to be a part of something so big and grand. But money mattered very little when people realized the only thing the ship builders skimped on were the lifeboats.

Regretfully, there were only half as many lifeboats as were needed for all of the passengers and crew. The lifeboats had actually been constructed and installed but were removed at the last minute to reduce the "clutter" on the first-class promenade deck. Primarily because they assumed they would never be needed.

It's interesting to point out that so-called "professionals" built the Titanic and claimed it was unsinkable, while others mocked an amateur as he built the Ark.

Without knowing the eventual result, the big, shiny ship may look like the perfect place to enjoy your retirement, but when you consider how both ended up, little doubt exists as to which ship and team I think you'd want to be on.

The "Good News" is that there's always a lifeboat waiting for you in Jesus Christ and you don't have to wait for disaster to strike in retirement to step in and start saving up treasures for heaven rather than earth!

Personal Thoughts & Notes:

About The Author

 Robert Laura is a pioneer in the psychology and social science of retirement. He is a five-time best-selling author, nationally syndicated columnist, and recognized presenter at retirement events across the country.

His work has reached millions with over 800 retirement articles and seven books including *Retirement Roots and The Retirement Devotional.* In addition to his own writings, he frequently appears in major business media outlets such as the Wall Street Journal, USA Today, CNBC, MarketWatch, New York Times, and more.

As a former social worker turned money manager and author, he has found that retirement is among the most fascinating, yet least understood, phases of life... particularly from a Biblical perspective.

As a result, he educates individuals, couples, groups, organizations and leaders on the need to develop a comprehensive retirement plan that puts God first, rather than money. In other words, to focus on Salvation, rather than savings.

Robert is also the founder of the Wealth & Wellness Group and the RetirementProject.org. He holds several designations including Certified Kingdom Advisor, Accredited Asset Management Specialist, Certified Mutual Fund Counselor, Chartered Retirement Planning Counselor, and Certified Professional Retirement Coach.

He is married to his amazing wife Amie, and together they have a blended family of four remarkable children: Connor, Ava, Luke, and Drake

Robert enjoys connecting with his readers. You are welcome to reach out to him personally at rl.robertlaura@gmail.com

Next Steps:

Visit RetirementMinistries.com to download a free copy of our *Retirement Prayers* guide.

There you can also check out our Retirement Roots Bible Study. This is an interactive, 6-part video series, where Robert helps individuals, couples, and groups develop a Christian Plan for everyday life in retirement. See also RetirementRoots.org, RightNowMedia.org, or Amazon.com